Henry Chadwick

The Baseball player's book of reference. : Containing the rules of the game for 1866 ; with an explanatory appendix ; full instructions for umpires ; instructions on scoring

Henry Chadwick

The Baseball player's book of reference. : Containing the rules of the game for 1866 ; with an explanatory appendix ; full instructions for umpires ; instructions on scoring

ISBN/EAN: 9783337156459

Printed in Europe, USA, Canada, Australia, Japan

Cover: Foto ©Andreas Hilbeck / pixelio.de

More available books at **www.hansebooks.com**

Errata.—By an error of the printer, pages 14 and 15 are duplicates of pages 10 and 11. It was impossible to correct this in the present edition; the following ones will be free from error.

A BASE BALL FIELD.

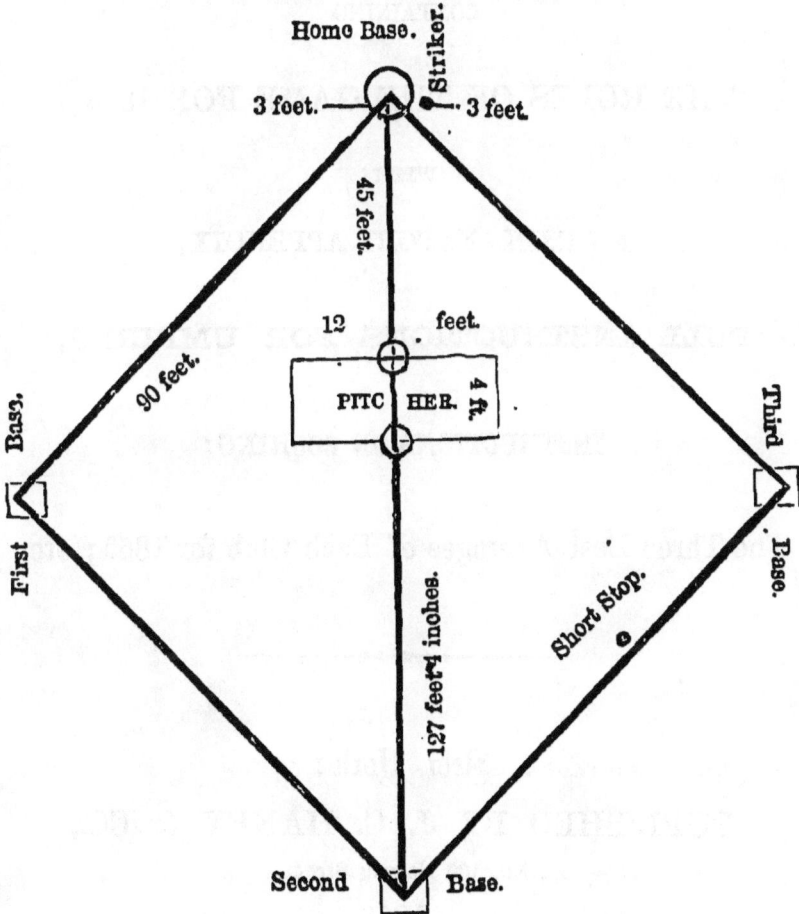

Catcher.

Scorers.

Umpire.

Home Base. Striker.

3 feet. 3 feet

45 feet.

12 feet.

PITC HER. 4 ft.

90 feet.

First Base.

Third Base.

127 feet 4 inches.

Short Stop.

Second Base.

Right Field.

Left Field.

Centre Field.

THE

BASE BALL PLAYER'S

BOOK OF REFERENCE.

CONTAINING

THE RULES OF THE GAME FOR 1866;

WITH

AN EXPLANATORY APPENDIX;

FULL INSTRUCTIONS FOR UMPIRES;

INSTRUCTIONS ON SCORING;

The Three Best Averages of Each Club for 1865; etc

———————⋆◆⋆———————

New York:

PUBLISHED BY J. C. HANEY & CO.,

. No. 109 Nassau Street.

1866.

INTRODUCTION.

THE NATIONAL SPORTS OF AMERICANS.

The physique of Americans has long been a vulnerable point for the attacks of foreigners on the weaknesses of our countrymen, and hitherto we have only too-well merited the palpable hits made by our healthy out-door-sport-loving cousins of England. Of late years, however, an improvement has been manifested in this respect in America, and a reformation has been introduced, which bids fair to remove this cause of complaint, and to bring us up to the physical standard of our forefathers, whose well exercised muscles enabled them to lay low the forests of the Western wilderness, and whose powers of endurance led them to withstand so manfully the fatigues and trials of the great seven years struggle for independence.

Among the most influential causes of this desirable reformation has been the establishment of a NATIONAL OUT-DOOR SPORT, something we were not possessed of even so late as ten years ago. Of course our sports must necessarily be, in the main, of foreign origin, as are the sports of England, of Norman or Roman descent; but we can as fairly claim for our American game of Base Ball—as played in accordance with the

rules of the " National Association of Base Ball Players"—an originality as an American institution, as the
English people can for their peculiarly national sport of
Horse Racing. Without further discussion on this
point, however, let it suffice that the game of Base Ball.
as perfected of late years, is undoubtedly an American
game. and one we can'now fairly claim as our national
out-door sport.

What Cricket is to an Englishman, Base Ball has become to an American. In England Cricket has more
devoted admirers and more ardent followers than any
recreation known to the English people. On the Cricket
field—and there only—the Peer and the Peasant meet
on equal terms ; the possession of courage, nerve, judgment, skill, endurance and activity alone giving the
palm of superiority. In fact, a more democratic institution does not exist in Europe than this self-same
Cricket ; and as regards its popularity, the records of
the thousands of games played each year, which in-
clude the names of Lords and Commoners, Divines and
Lawyers, Legislators and Artizans, and Literateurs as
well as Mechanics and Laborers, shows how great a hold
it has on the people. If this is the characteristic of
Cricket in aristocratic and monarchical England, how
much more will the same characteristics mark Base
Ball in democratic and republican America ?

Unreflecting and prejudiced individuals, who never
look beneath the surface of things, may regard both
Cricket and Base Ball " as very good things for boys,

perhaps," or to "pass away an idle hour or so on a holiday ;" but those who intelligently investigate subjects in regard to cause and effect, see in both these games, but especially in Base Ball, the means to an end which has been sought for in vain for years past, on this side the Atlantic. As a means of cultivating the physical powers, Base Ball is one of the most commendable exercises in vogue. As a remedy for many of the evils resulting from the immoral associations the boys and young men of our cities are apt to become connected with, the game merits the endorsement of every clergyman in the country ; and we are gratified to notice that one eminent preacher has publicly commended Base Ball from the pulpit, the Rev. C. H. Everett, of Brooklyn, in a sermon he delivered in 1865, on Physical Education, having made a special allusion to Base Ball as a game "whose regulations are calculated to prevent the ill-feelings engendered by other games, and one, moreover, which serves to attract our young men from places of bad repute, and to supply in place thereof the right kind of recreation and exercise." This opinion has been practically endorsed by several clergymen of Philadelphia, who, the same year, formed themselves into a Base Ball club for purposes of moral and healthful recreation, in imitation of hundreds of their brother clergymen of England, who take such delight in playing Cricket with their parishioners on the "commons" or "greens" of the villages, over which they have pastoral control.

But one of the strongest aids to the popularity of Base Ball, lays in the fact that it is a game—and about the only one, by-the-way—which can be countenanced and patronized by the fair sex. American ladies have hitherto been shut out from all the pleasures incident to games, in which contests are entered upon for the palm of superiority in courage, activity, nerve, judgment, and manly skill, by the low character of the surroundings of most of the sports and pastimes men indulge in. In Base Ball, however, we have an exception in favor of the ladies, and one, too, they have not been slow to avail themselves of, as the presence of the fair sex by hundreds at a time at the leading contests of the past five or six seasons fully testifies. If our National Pastime had no other recommendation than this, this alone would suffice to give it a popularity no other re-creation could reach or compete with, in the estimation of Americans. To conclude our introduction, however, we have to state that, whether Base Ball be regarded as a desirable means of physical exercise, an exciting game for the masses, a recreation for the refined classes of the community, or an out-door sport devoid of every objectionable attribute the most fastidious moralist could charge it with possessing, it is equally to be com-mended to the patronage of every reputable citizen, North, East, South and West, as the most suitable game for the national out-door sport of the American people

BASE BALL PLAYERS'

BOOK OF REFERENCE.

The Ball.

SEC. 1. The ball must weigh not less than five and one-half, nor more than five and three-fourths ounces, avoirdupois. It must measure not less than nine and one-half, nor more than nine and three-fourths inches in circumference. It must be composed of India rubber and yarn, and covered with leather, and, in all match games, shall be furnished by the challenging club, and become the property of the winning club as a trophy of victory.

[In selecting a ball for a match, the one nine and one-half inches in circumference, and five and three-quarters ounces in weight, will be found the most elastic, and the best for batting purposes, because the yarn and rubber in it is wound tighter than in balls measuring more and weighing less. In match games, if you send a challenge to a club, you have to supply the first ball and they the second, each supplying one for the third, the new ball of the two going to the winning club.]

The Bat.

SEC. 2. The bat must be round, and must not exceed two and a half inches in diameter in the thickest part. It must be made of wood, and may be of any length to suit the striker.

[The lighter the bat, provided the wood is of a tough kind, the better. It is almost impossible to hit quick enough for swift pitching with a heavy bat, unless the batsman is very strong in the arms. Strength in the wrists is the main thing in batting.]

The Bases.

SEC. 3. The bases must be four in number, placed at equal distances from each other, and securely fastened upon each corner of a square, whose sides are respectively thirty yards. They must be so constructed as to be distinctly seen by the umpire, and must cover a space equal to one square foot of surface. The first, second and third bases shall be canvas bags, painted white, and filled with some soft material, the home base and pitcher's point to be each marked by a flat, circular iron plate, painted or enameled white.

[There have been several patent-bases introduced, those used on the Union ball grounds, Brooklyn, being the best. As a general thing, the canvas bag strapped round the centre with a strong leather band will be found as serviceable as any.]

The Home Base.

SEC. 4. The base from which the ball is struck shall be designated the Home Base, and must be directly opposite the second base; the first base must always be that upon the right hand, and the third base that upon the left hand side of the striker, when occupying his position at the Home Base. And in all match games a line connecting the home and first base and the home and third base, shall be marked by the use of chalk, or other suitable material, so as to be distinctly seen by the umpire.

[It is very necessary that the rule in regard to having chalk lines made, should be enforced, as it greatly assists the Umpire in deciding on foul balls, besides making it plain to all present that the decisions are correct. The home-base quoit should be *flat*, as the rule requires, and not rising in the centre, as some do; for when a ball touches the latter, instead of rebounding for the catcher, as it would do if the base were flat, it flies off at a tangent, and allows of bases being run on the passed ball.]

The Pitcher's Position.

SEC. 5. The pitcher's position shall be designated by two lines, four yards in length, drawn at right angles to a line from home to second base, having their centres upon that line at two fixed iron plates, placed at points fifteen and sixteen and one-third yards distant from the home base.   The pitcher must stand within the lines, and must deliver the ball as near as possible over the centre of the home base, and for the striker.

[The term "pitched for the striker" means balls pitched within his legitimate reach—that is, the length of his bat from him—and not balls which the striker's whim or fancy may call for. If the batsman is in the habit of striking a very low or very high ball, then the pitcher must pitch the ball to suit his peculiar style, viz.: "for the striker;" but he is not required so to pitch unless the batsman is in the habit of striking at balls of the kind, or in other words, the batsman cannot demand a low ball if he is in the habit of striking one hip high.]

Delivering Unfair Balls.

Sec. 6. Should the pitcher repeatedly fail to deliver to the striker fair balls, for the apparent purpose of delaying the game, or for any cause, the umpire, after warning him, shall call one ball, and if the pitcher persists in such action, two and three balls; when three balls shall have been called, the striker shall take the first base ; and should any base be occupied at that time, each player occupying it or them shall take one base without being put out.

[Before balls are called on a pitcher, he must be warned by the umpire; but only one warning is necessary for each striker. If two balls are pitched unfairly, after such warning, then "one ball" should be called, and if after that, one unfair ball be delivered, then "two

balls" and " three balls" should be called. A little latitude should be allowed in the first innings, but not
afterward. A pitcher " repeatedly" fails if he fails twice
in succession ; and he " persists" in his unfair delivery if
he pitch one ball after the first penalty has been im-
posed.]

Pitching.—Baulks.

SEC. 7. The ball must be pitched, not jerked
or thrown, to the bat ; and whenever the
pitcher moves with the apparent purpose or
pretension to deliver the ball, he shall so deliver it, and must have neither foot in advance
of the front line or off the ground at the time
of delivering the ball ; and if he fails in either
of these particulars, then it shall be declared
a baulk.

[A "pitched" ball is one that reaches the batsman
without touching the ground. If it touches the ground
it becomes a "bowled" ball. A "jerked" ball is a ball
delivered swiftly from the hand by the arm first touching the side of the pitcher ; if the arm does not touch
his side, the ball is not "jerked." A ball can be thrown
under hand as well as over the shoulder ; but it cannot
be thrown with a straight arm. Therefore, if the pitcher
keeps a straight arm, that is, without bending his elbow,
he does not throw the ball. The sentence, "time of delivering the ball," has been interpreted by the Committee
on Rules and Regulations of the National Association,
to mean the period when the last movement of the arm
is made in delivering the ball ; and, consequently, if
either foot of the pitcher be off the ground when this
movement is made—it being nearly simultaneous with

the ball leaving the hand of the pitcher—umpires must declare a baulk without being appealed to.]

Rule for Players When a Baulk is Made.

SEC. 8. When a baulk is made by the pitcher, every player running the bases is entitled to one base without being put out.

[A "player running the bases" is one who has made his first base ; until he makes the first base he is considered the striker and as such is not entitled to a base when a baulk is made.]

Foul and Fair Balls.

SEC. 9. If the ball, from a stroke of the bat, first touches the ground, the person of a player or any other object, behind the range of home and the first base, or home and the third base, it shall be termed foul, and must be so declared by the umpire, unasked. If the ball first touches the ground, either upon, or in front of the range of those bases, it shall be considered fair.

[Special rules are requisite in all cases when there are peculiarities of a ground to interfere with fielding operations, such as a tree, a house or a fence in the way In such cases, if a foul ball is caught on the fly from a tree, it counts only as a bound catch, and if a fair ball is held on the fly on a re-bound from a fence or a house it is no catch unless mutually agreed to be so considered before the game is commenced.]

Making the Home Base.

SEC. 10. A player making the home base shall be entitled to score one run.

[Home runs are not recognized by the rules. Custom considers a home run as being made, if the home base is reached before the ball passes the line of the home base from the outer field, provided the batsman has not been obliged to stop on any base for fear of being put out. A " clean home run"—and none other should be counted in the score—is a run made from home to home, from a hit made to long field beyond the reach of the out-fielders.]

Balls Struck at and Missed.

SEC. 11. If three balls are struck at, and missed, and the last one is not caught, either flying or upon the first bound, it shall be considered fair, and the striker must attempt to make his run.

[The Committee of Rules have decided that the bound catch in this instance shall be considered in the light of a foul ball, as far as the catch is concerned, from the fact of its striking the ground back of the home base.]

A Foul Ball Caught Puts the Striker Out.

SEC. 12. The striker is out if a foul ball is caught, either before touching the ground, or upon the first bound.

[If a " foul fly" is nursed by one fielder, and another catches the ball from his hands or person before it touches the ground, such a catch is a foul bound catch and counts.]

Bound Catch of a Foul Ball.

SEC. 13. Or, if three balls are struck at and missed, and the last is caught, either before touching the ground, or upon the first bound.

[Scorers should record the batsman as "struck out" in this instance, whether he is caught out by the catcher or put out at first base after the bound catch, has been made.]

A Fair Ball made Foul.

SEC. 14. Or, if a fair ball is struck, and the ball is caught without having touched the ground.

[The person of a player, a tree, a fence, or a building, are all regarded as "the ground" in this instance, and if the ball touches either before it is caught, the catch does not count.]

Ball Held by Adversary upon First Base.

SEC. 15. Or, if a fair ball is struck, and the ball is held by an adversary on first base, before the striker touches that base.

[It should be distinctly understood by all that the ball must be held on the first base "before" the striker touches it, or he is not out; if, at the same time, he is not out. It must be palpable that the ball was held before the base was touched, or the player making the base is not out.]

Players Touched by the Ball While Running.

SEC. 16. Any player running the bases is out if at any time he is touched by the ball while in play in the hands of an adversary, without some part of his person being on the base.

[A player makes his base if he touches the base-bag, no matter whether the base bag is in its position or not. That alone is considered the "base."]

No Base can be Made on a Foul Ball.

SEC. 17. No ace or base can be made upon a foul ball ; such a ball shall be considered dead, and not in play until it shall first have been settled in the hands of the pitcher. In such cases players running bases shall return to them, and may be put out in so returning in the same manner as the striker when running to the first base.

[The player running the bases must return to the base he left when the ball was struck, and *remain upon it* until the ball is "settled" in the hands of the pitcher, after which he can leave his base.]

Running Bases.

SEC. 18. No ace nor base can be made when a fair ball has been caught without having touched the ground ; such a ball shall be conthe ball leaving the hand of the pitcher—umpires must declare a baulk without being appealed to.]

Rule for Players When a Baulk is Made.

Sec. 8. When a baulk is made by the pitcher, every player running the bases is entitled to one base without being put out.

[The striker cannot take a base on a baulk for the reason that he is not a player running the bases until he has struck a fair ball.]

Foul and Fair Balls.

Sec. 9. If the ball, from a stroke of the bat, first touches the ground, the person of a player or any other object, behind the range of home and the first base, or home and the third base, it shall be termed foul, and must be so declared by the umpire, unasked. If the ball first touches the ground, either upon, or in front of the range of those bases, it shall be considered fair.

[Special rules are requisite in all cases where there are peculiarities of a ground to interfere with fielding operations, such as a tree, a house or a fence in the way. In such cases, if a foul ball is caught on the fly from a tree, it counts only as a bound catch, and if a fair ball is held on the fly on a re-bound from a fence or a house, it is no catch unless mutually agreed to be so considered before the game is commenced.]

Making the Home Base.

SEC. 10. A player making the home base shall be entitled to score one run.

[Home runs are not recognized by the rules. Custom considers a home run as being made, if the home base is reached before the ball passes the line of the home base from the outer field, provided the batsman has not been obliged to stop on any base to avoid being put out. A "clean home run"—and none other should be counted in the score—is a run made from home to home, from a hit made to long-field beyond the reach of the out-fielders.]

Balls Struck at and Missed.

SEC. 11. If three balls are struck at, and missed, and the last one is not caught, either flying or upon the first bound, it shall be considered fair, and the striker must attempt to make his run.

[The Committee of Rules have decided that the bound catch in this instance shall be considered in the light of a foul ball, as far as the catch is concerned, from the fact of its striking the ground back of the home base.]

A Foul Ball Caught Puts the Striker Out.

SEC. 12. The striker is out if a foul ball is caught, either before touching the ground, or upon the first bound.

[If a "foul fly" is missed by one fielder, and another

catches the ball from his hands or person before it touches the ground, such a catch counts.]

Bound Catch of a Foul Ball.

SEC. 13. Or, if three balls are struck at and missed, and the last is caught, either before touching the ground, or upon the first bound.

[Scorers should record the batsman as "struck out" in this instance, whether he is caught out by the catcher or put out at first base after the bound catch has been missed.]

A Fair Ball on the Fly.

SEC. 14. Or, if a fair ball is struck, and the ball is caught without having touched the ground.

[A tree, a fence, or a building, are all regarded as "the ground" in this instance, and if the ball touches either before it is caught, the catch does not count, except in the case of a foul ball.]

Ball Held by Adversary upon First Base.

SEC. 15. Or, if a fair ball is struck, and the ball is held by an adversary on first base, before the striker touches that base.

[It should be distinctly understood by all that the ball must be held on the first base "before" the striker touches it, or he is not out; if, at the same time, he is not out. It must be palpable that the ball was held before the base was touched, or the player making the base is not out.]

Players Touched by the Ball while Running.

SEC. 16. Any player running the bases is out if at any time he is touched by the ball while in play in the hands of an adversary, without some part of his person being on the base.

[A player makes his base if he touches the base-bag, no matter whether the base-bag is in its position or not. That alone is considered the "base."]

No Base can be made on a Foul Ball.

SEC. 17. No ace or base can be made upon a foul ball ; such a ball shall be considered dead, and not in play until it shall first have been settled in the hands of the pitcher. In such cases players running bases shall return to them, and may be put out in so returning in the same manner as the striker when running to the first base;

[The player running the bases must return to the base he left when the ball was struck, and *remain upon it* until the ball is "settled" in the hands of the pitcher, after which he can leave his base.]

Running Bases.

SEC. 18. No ace nor base can be made when a fair ball has been caught without having touched the ground ; such a ball shall be considered alive and in play. In such cases play-ers running bases shall return to them, and may be put out in so returning, in the same manner as the striker when running to first base ; but players, when balls are so caught, may run their bases immediately after the ball has been settled in the hands of the player catching it.

[In the case of fair balls taken on the fly, a player, running his bases when the ball is struck, must return to the base he left, and touch it, and wait on it until the ball is settled in the hands of the fielder catching it ; after which he can again run for the next base without waiting for the ball to go to the pitcher.]

Position of Strikers.—Players must Strike in Rotation.

SEC. 19. The striker must stand on a line drawn through the centre of the home base, not exceeding in length three feet from either side thereof, and parallel with the line occu-pied by the pitcher. He shall be considered the striker until he has made the first base. Players must strike in regular rotation, and, after the first innings is played, the turn com-mences with the player who stands on the list next to the one who lost the third hand.

[This standing on the line of his position is quite im-portant. In the first place the striker has no right to avail himself of the advantage derived from standing back of the line of his position, thereby increasing the

distance between himself and the pitcher and obtaining
a better opportunity of judging the ball; besides which,
a poorly hit ball which would strike the ground in front
of the home base—if the batsman stood on the line of
his base—and lead to his being put out, is changed to a
foul ball by his standing back of his base, and he thereby escapes the penalty of his poor batting. Another
fact is, the striker, by not standing on the line in ques
tion, deprives himself of the right to demand fair balls
from the pitcher.]—See " Duties of Umpire."

Vacating Bases.—Putting Players Out.

SEC. 20. Players must make their bases in
the order of striking ; and when a fair ball is
struck, and not caught flying, the first base
must be vacated, as also the second and third
bases, if they are occupied at the same time.
Players may be put out on any base, under
these circumstances, in the same manner as the
striker when running to the first base.

[Players running bases can only be forced to leave
their bases when each base is occupied, and the striker
hits a fair ball. No player can run another off a base
under any other circumstances.]

Bases Must be Touched.—Order of Bases.

SEC. 21. Players running bases must touch
them ; and, so far as possible, keep upon the
direct line between them ; and must touch
them in the following order ; first, second,
third and home ; and if returning must reverse this order ; and should any player run

three feet out of this line, for the purpose of avoiding the ball in the hands of an adversary, he shall be declared out.

[A player running his bases can only be decided out by the Umpire for running out of the line of the bases to avoid the ball. If he does so to avoid interfering with a fielder, he does not infringe the rule. If he fails to touch a base he must return to it, and must be touched with the ball before he does return, in order to put him out.]

Preventing a Player Catching a Ball.

SEC. 22. Any player, who shall intentionally prevent an adversary from catching or fielding the ball, shall be declared out.

[The word "intentionally," in these rules, refers to actions which might have been avoided. Thus, if a fielder happens to be standing on the line of a base to catch a falling ball, the player has no right to run up against him because he is between him and the base, for he can run a foot or two to one side and not thereby be prevented from reaching his base by the effort of the fielder to catch the ball. So in regard to a base player taking a ball from a fielder, he having no right to stand between the player and the base when the ball could be equally well taken by standing out of the way of his adversary. In these instances the obstruction should be regarded as intentional, from the fact that it might readily have been avoided.]

Unfair Base Play.

SEC. 23. If the player is prevented from making a base, by the intentional obstruction of an adversary, he shall be entitled to that base, and not be put out.

[If the ball be stopped by a crowd at the back of either the first or third base, the ball must be returned to the pitcher before it can be used to put a player out.]

Stopping the Ball.—Non-Players.

SEC. 24. If an adversary stops the ball with his hat or cap, or if a ball be stopped by any person not engaged in the game, or if it be taken from the hands of any one not engaged in the game, no player can be put out unless the ball shall first have been settled in the hands of the pitcher.

[A ball held in the lap of a fielder, or between his knees, or on his feet before it touches the ground it is a fair catch.]

Striker Out.

SEC. 25. If a ball, from the stroke of a bat, is held under any other circumstances than as enumerated in Section 24, and without having touched the ground, the striker is out.

[Of course, if the striker makes his first base—thereby ceasing to be the striker—and is touched with the ball in trying to make his second base, or either of the other bases, the player running home before him scores his run; but the home base, in such an instance as this, must be reached before the player is put out, or the run does not count.]

Running Home after the Striker is Out.

SEC. 26. If two hands are already out, no player running home at the time the ball is struck can make a *run to count in the score of the game* if the striker is put out.

[The moment the third hand is out no player running home can count his run if the home base is touched after the player is put out.]

Innings Concluded when Third Hand is Out.

SEC. 27. An innings must be concluded at the time the third hand is put out.

[Any number of innings can be played after the ninth inning, until one party or the other takes the lead, provided the score is even at the close of the ninth inning.]

What Concludes the Game.

SEC. 28. The game shall consist of nine innings to each side, when, should the number of runs be equal, the play shall be continued, until a majority of runs, upon an equal number of innings, shall be declared, which shall couclude the game.

[Any less number than five innings does not constitute a game. If any number of innings have been played between five and nine, and the last play is not completed on account of darkness or rain, the result of the last even innings played decides a game. Thus if five innings have been played and one side have played their sixth, and the other side have two hands out on their sixth inning, and it becomes too dark for the umpire to see the ball, or too wet from rain for play to be continued, and the game be "called" by the umpire, the score of the five innings played decides the contest.]

Regulations of Matches.

SEC. 29. In playing all matches, nine players from each club shall constitute a full field, and they must have been regular members of the club which they represent, and of no other club, *either in or out of the National Association*, for thirty days prior to the match. No change or substitution shall be made after the game has been commenced, unless for reasons of illness or injury. Position of players and of innings shall be determined by captains previously appointed for that purpose by the respective clubs.

[The above rule does not exclude members of cricket clubs, as cricket is a different game. But it excludes members of all base ball clubs, whether of the senior or junior fraternity, or of clubs in or out of the National Association. No player can be changed unless for just cause, such as positive inability to play by reason of illness or serious injury. According to the new rule (Section 38) mutual consent cannot permit one player to be substituted for another, except for the causes indicated. Therefore, if any particular player is wanted and he is not on hand at the time the game begins, the side he belongs to must play eight men.]

Duties of the Umpire.

SEC. 30. The umpire shall take care that the regulations respecting the ball, bats, bases, and the pitcher's and striker's position are strictly observed. He shall be the judge of fair and unfair play, and shall determine all disputes and differences which may occur during the game; he shall take special care to declare all foul balls and baulks immediately upon their occurrence, unasked, in a distinct and audible manner. He shall, in every instance, before leaving the ground, declare the winning club, and shall record his decision in the books of the scorers.

[For comments on the duties of the Umpire, see "Instructions for Umpires."

Selection of Umpire and Scorers.

SEC. 31. In all matches the umpire shall be selected by the captains of the respective sides, and shall perform all the duties enumerated in Section 28, except recording the game, which shall be done by two scorers, one of whom shall be appointed by each of the contending clubs.

[See comments on umpires, &c.]

Bets by Umpires and Players Illegal.

SEC. 32. No person engaged in a match, either as umpire, scorer or player, shall be directly or indirectly interested in any bets upon the game. Neither umpire, scorer, nor player shall be changed during a match, unless with the consent of both parties (except for a violation of this law) except as provided in Section 29, and then the umpire may dismiss any transgressors.

[The sentence, " consent of both parties," in the above rule, refers only to a change rendered necessary by reason of " illness or injury." Rule 29 expressly reads, " no change or substitution shall be made after the game has been commenced, unless for reasons of illness or injury, and not then without the consent of both parties" as referred to in the above rule. This rule, as far as it prohibits betting, has hitherto been a dead letter. This year more care will be taken to observe the rule, for those who bet large sums on the leading contests of the season intend to dispute the loss of their bets in all cases wherein this rule is not observed ; and they will have the right—according to the best sporting authority—to hold the stake holder responsible in every instance in which he pays over the stake to the winner when this rule has been broken ; for under such circumstances the wager is not fairly won.]

When Play Shall be Suspended.

SEC. 33. The umpire in any match shall determine when play shall be suspended ; and if the game cannot be concluded, it shall be decided by the last even innings, provided five innings have been played, and the party having the greatest number of runs shall be declared the winner.

Balls Knocked Beyond Bounds.

SEC. 34. Clubs may adopt such rules respecting balls knocked beyond or outside the bounds of the field, as the circumstances of the ground may demand ; and these rules shall govern all matches played upon the ground, provided that they are distinctly made known to every player and umpire previous to the commencement of the game.

[The adoption of special rules referred to in this section applies only to rules governing catches made from trees, fences or buildings, and these do not apply unless a mutual understanding is had previous to the commencement of the game.]

Communicating with the Umpire.

SEC. 35. No person shall be permitted to approach or to speak with the umpire, scorers, or players, or in any manner to interrupt or interfere during the progress of the game, unless by special request of the umpire.

[The habit that players have of standing talking near the umpire should be put a stop to. The umpire needs all his wits about him to attend to his duties, and every·

thing calculated to distract his attention from the game should be avoided.]

Umpires and Scorers to be Members of a Club.

SEC. 36. No person shall be permitted to act as umpire or scorer in any match unless he shall be a member of a Base Ball Club governed by these rules.

[This is one of the rules which is seldom observed. Every club should appoint a regular scorer for the season, and he should be competent to record the fielding as well as batting score of the game. Until this is done, a full analysis of the season's play of a club cannot be obtained.]

Play to be Called at the Time Appointed.

SEC. 37. Whenever a match shall have been determined upon between two clubs, play shall be called at the exact hour appointed ; and should either party fail to produce their players within fifteen minutes thereafter, the party so failing shall admit a defeat.

[It is to be hoped that this rule will be more strictly observed than it hitherto has been. When clubs appoint a time for calling the game it should be promptly proceeded with after the time allowed by the rule has expired.]

Games Considered Null and Void.

SEC. 38. Any match game played by any

club in contravention of the rules adopted by this Association, shall be considered null and void, and shall not be counted in the list of match games won or lost, except a game be delayed by rain beyond the time appointed to commence the same. Any match game can be put off by mutual consent of the parties about engaging in the game. No match game shall be commenced in the rain.

[This is a new rule, and was designed to obviate the difficulty attending upon the repudiation of any rule of the game any two clubs may mutually agree to ignore. Thus, for instance, any two clubs agreeing to allow a member of either club to play in a match who has not been a member for thirty days previous to a match, by this rule cannot claim the ball won, or count the match played as a regular game. The exception made in case of rain refers to that rule which requires a game to commence within fifteen minutes of the time appointed.]

No one in Arrears Allowed to Play.

SEC. 39. No person who shall be in arrears to any other club, or who shall at any time receive compensation for his services as player, shall be competent to play in any match.

Failure of the Striker to Strike.

[Section 40 is a rule that should be strictly enforced, as it refers to a part of the game that is oft-times a very tedious and annoying feature. How often do we see the striker, the moment his predecessor has made his first base, stand still at the home base and await the moment when the player on the first base can avail himself of the failure of either the pitcher or catcher to hold the ball while tossing it backward and forward to each other. Some catchers—chiefly among boys, however—actually stand to the home base purposely for this style of game; and even when the pitcher and catcher are inclined to do their duty, the batsmam is not, and the latter is frequently allowed to stop the progress of the game by his refusal to strike at good balls, under the plea that they do not suit him, when it is apparent to all that he simply wants to allow his partner to get to his second base. In every respect it is preferable to play the game manfully and without resorting to any such trickery as this, which not only tires the spectator, but detracts from the merit of the game itself. Even under the new rule of pitching, this unfair play was practiced last season. It is to be hoped that umpires will do their duty this year, and put an entire stop to it, which they have the power to do.]

What Decides a Match.

SEC. 41. Every match hereafter made shall be decided by the best two games out of three, unless a single game shall be mutually agreed upon by the contesting clubs.

THE POSITION OF UMPIRE.

Its Duties, &c.

THE QUALIFICATIONS OF AN UMPIRE.—It is almost unnecessary to remark that the first duty of an Umpire is to enforce the rules of the game with the strictest impartiality. An all-important requisite, too, is familiarity with every point of the game. Experience has shown the fallacy of the opinion that because a man happens to be an excellent player, he must necessarily make a good Umpire. We have seen too many instances in which almost the very reverse has been the case, to adopt that as a rule. It requires a man of considerable moral courage to act impartially in the position, and decision of character, coolness of judgment and quickness in observation are also necessary qualifications. These several characteristics few possess, and consequently thoroughly competent Umpires are to be found few and far between.

SELECTING AN UMPIRE.—In selecting an umpire, choose the man you know to be " a true man," that is, one who, howsoever he may err in judgment, decides a point according to his honest and unprejudiced opinion. Such a one is preferable to any other, who, lacking this quality, possesses every other attribute of a competent judge.

WHO CAN ACT AS AN UMPIRE.—No man can act as an Umpire in a match, who is not a member of a club belonging to the National Association.

FAVORS CONFERRED BY UMPIRES.—Contesting nines and their friends invariably forget, in their comments on the decisions of Umpires, that the Umpire is the *obliging* party, and the players his debtors. Without an Umpire no game can be played ; and inasmuch as the position of Umpire, in a base ball match, must always be an office unpaid for and honorary in its character, unless all unpleasantness connected with the position, and all objections to occupying it, are removed, it will be difficult to obtain any one willing to assume the office who is worthy and competent to act.

AVOID PREJUDICING AN UMPIRE.—If an umpire commits an error, finding fault with him will not improve his judgment ; on the contrary it is very likely to prejudice him against the parties censuring him. The best way, when errors are committed, is to remember that the umpire is doing your club a favor in acting in the position, and to credit him with endeavoring to do his best to oblige. Above all, remember that your Captain, as your representative, consented to his occupying the position, and that therefore he is not acting as Umpire in opposition to the wishes of your club.

QUESTIONING DECISIONS.—In no case has any player of a nine a right to question the decision of an Umpire except the captain, and he only in the form of soliciting information in regard to a disputed point, and not as questioning the Umpire's judgment. The captain alone is the spokesman of the nine. If a player should become cognizant of an error of the Umpire's requiring explanation, as sometimes occurs, let him call " Time," and point out the error to the captain. This should be done, however, only in rare instances, and where the error committed is a palpable one in interpreting the rules, and not an error of judgment. As a general rule, however, *silent acquiescence* in every decision of the Umpire is the best policy, as it certainly is the one most characteristic of gentlemanly players.

THE GOLDEN RULE IN UMPIRING.—The Umpire should invariably render his decision in accordance with the *first impressions* of the point of play, made on his mind. If he hesitates at all, the influence of any particular bias he may have will affect his judgment, and very likely make his decision a partial one. Be prompt, therefore, to decide according to the very first impression made. Promptness in deciding is strong testimony in favor of impartial judgment, and is always satisfactory to contestants.

THE DUTIES OF UMPIRES.

WHAT THE LAW SAYS.

"SEC. 30. The umpire shall take care that the regulations respecting the ball, bats, bases, and the pitcher's and striker's position are strictly observed. He shall be the judge of fair and unfair play, and shall determine all disputes and differences which may occur during the game. He shall take special care to declare all foul balls and baulks immediately upon their occurrence, unasked, in a distinct and audible manner. He shall, in every instance, before leaving the ground, declare the winning club, and shall record his decision in the books of the scorers."

THE SIZE OF THE BALL.—Before "play" is called, the Umpire should see that the *ball*, to be played with, is of the regulation size and weight, viz., not more than $5\frac{3}{4}$ oz. in weight, nor less than $9\frac{1}{2}$ inches in circumference

THE FOUL BALL LINES AND POSTS.—He should also see that the *Foul Ball Posts* are in position, and especially that the rule requiring *chalk lines*, from home to first base and home to third, be complied with.

THE PITCHER'S POSITION.—He should also see that the lines of the pitcher's position are properly laid down, viz., forty five feet from the home base for the front line, and four feet further for the back line ; with a line of twelve feet in length for the position ; and within this space the pitcher must stand, keeping both feet on the ground, from the time he prepares to deliver the ball, until it leaves his hand.

THE STRIKER'S POSITION.—He should see that the strikcr, when he takes his position to strike, has one foot on the line of his position. This is a very important rule, and yet it is one that few Umpires have enforced hitherto. In the first place, if the striker is permitted to stand two or three feet back of the home base, and he strikes a ball nearly perpendicular to the ground, the ball touches the ground back of the home base and at once becomes a foul ball, and in such cases the rebound is generally one making a catch difficult. Now, the very same ball, struck by the batsman while in his proper position, viz., with one foot on the line of the home base, would invariably be a fair ball, and one that would lead to his being easily put out at first base. It will be seen, therefore, that by not standing on the line of his position he gains an advantage he is not entitled to. Again, if the striker be not in his proper position, he cannot legally insist upon fair balls being delivered to him ; and as the Umpire is the sole judge of fair and unfair play, and this failure of the striker to stand on the line of the position is unfair play, the Umpire should not inflict any penalty upon the pitcher for failing to deliver fair balls to him while he is thus out of his place.

CALLING FOUL BALLS.—He should call foul balls in a loud tone of voice, especially when a player is running his bases. When a ball is struck high in the air, and it is doubtful whether it will fall fair or foul, the Umpire should wait until the ball touches the ground or the person of a player before he calls "foul," for until it does so touch the ground, it really is not a foul ball. When the ball is "tipped" he can call it foul more promptly than when struck high in the air.

SILENCE FOR FAIR BALLS.—The Umpire should keep silent when a fair ball is struck, but if asked if it be a fair ball, he can, of course, say so ; but he is not required to call fair balls.

THE SPECIAL RULES OF A BALL GROUND.—The Umpire, before calling "play," should see that the Captains of the contesting sides are mutually agreed upon what the rules of the ground are for the match.   Thus, for instance, that a ball going over a fence shall give but one base, or that a ball taken on the fly from a tree, or the roof of a house, or the side of a fence, shall be regarded as a bound catch and only legitimate in the case of a foul ball ; or that a ball passing the catcher, and being stopped by a fence too close to the home base, shall give one base, etc.

CALLING BALLS AND STRIKES.

CALLING BALLS ON PITCHERS.—This has hitherto been one of the most difficult duties of an Umpire ; a study of these rules, however, will simplify matters considerably in this respect.   The Umpire should first instruct himself in regard to the definition of unfair balls, and the following rules will give him the required information.

UNFAIRLY PITCHED BALLS.—A ball that strikes the ground in front of the home base is not a fair ball, as in the first place, by striking the ground, before reaching the batsman, it becomes a "bowled" ball, and, secondly, because it is not pitched "over the home base and for the striker ;" for, unless it goes over the home base before touching the ground it is not "pitched" but "bowled" over, and unless so pitched it cannot be, for the striker.

A ball that is pitched on the side opposite to that the batsman habitually strikes from, is not a foul ball, because not pitched "for the striker."

A ball that is pitched so as to hit the striker—provided he is standing in his legitimate position, viz., with one foot on the line of the home base—is not a fair one for the same reason. The striker should, however, stand far enough from the base to admit of the ball being pitched over it without its striking him.

Balls, too, which are pitched beyond the legitimate reach of the batsman, either in front of him or over his head are, for the same reason, not fair balls.

Certainly, all of the above balls are unfairly delivered, and can be legitimately regarded by the Umpire as balls to be called whenever pitched, provided due warning has been given the pitcher. Should the striker not stand in his position, as required by the 19th section of the rules, the Umpire is not required to call any of the above delivered balls as unfair balls.

CALLING STRIKES.—The Umpire should be as strict in inflicting the penalty of the law on a batsman for failing to strike at fair balls for any special object, as he is in regard to the pitcher for unfair delivery. Hitherto impartial justice has not been the rule in this respect. When the striker is in his regular position, and fair balls are delivered to him—that is, balls within his legitimate reach, and "as near as possible over the home base," and "for the striker"—the Umpire, after warning him, should unhesitatingly call "strikes" on him. In judging of the action of the striker in this matter, and in inflicting the penalty of the law, the same rules apply as in the case of calling balls, viz., in interpreting the words "repeatedly" and "persists." Should the striker not stand on the base line, however, every ball, passing at all near him, should be regarded as fair, and if he fails to strike at such ball, "strikes" should be called on him. No law breaker himself can justly call for punishment on a similar offender.

No Cause Justifies Unfair Delivery.—The Umpire should bear in mind that the words of the rule, in reference to a failure to deliver fair balls, are, "or for any cause." Therefore he should disregard the fact of the unfair pitching being unintentional, inasmuch as inability to deliver fair balls, whether arising from lack of skill in accuracy of delivery, or from too great a desire to pitch swiftly, is to be regarded as just cause for inflicting the penalty, as much so as wilfully unfair delivery would be.

Pitching for the Striker.—The pitcher is required to deliver the ball "as near as possible over the centre of the home base" and "for the striker." The words "for the striker" are rather indefinite for the wording of an arbitrary rule, but the correct interpretation is, that the pitcher must deliver to the batsman balls within the *legitimate* reach of his bat. What this legitimate reach is has been shown under the head of "Unfair Pitched Balls." Every experienced batsman has a peculiar and favorite style of hitting. Brinkerhoff—formerly of the Eagle club—could never hit a ball higher than a foot from the ground. P. O'Brien takes one very readily as high as his head. The generality of batsmen, however, require them about hip high. Now, this peculiarity of hitting is well known to all in the club a player belongs to, and can readily be ascertained, and when the Umpire knows what ball the batsman is in the habit of striking at, he is then able to judge what a ball "for the striker" should be. This done, he should not allow a player to suit his particular whim or fancy in the matter, but should consider every ball "for the striker" that is pitched within reasonable distance of the point the batsman is in the habit of requiring a ball to be pitched to him. When a player is running his bases, and the period of the game is a critical one as regards the issue of the contest, we frequently find that a batsman who is in the habit of striking at balls hip high, will call for a "low ball," in the hope that the pitcher, in his efforts to deliver a low ball, will pitch one likely to pass the catcher, in which case bases can be run by the player, that being the object of the striker in calling for "a low ball." This, of course, the striker has no right to do, and therefore the Umpire cannot require a pitcher to send in such ball, unless the fact is well known that the batsman is in the habit of striking at low balls.

WARNING PLAYERS.—In regard to the warning required to be given in cases of calling "balls" and "strikes," once being warned, for each striker, is sufficient. "Ball to the bat" is all the warning necessary in regard to unfair delivery in pitching, and any simple word of caution in reference to the penalty likely to be incurred, is all that is requisite in the case of "strikes."

ON BAULKING.

CALLING BAULKS.—The point next in importance to that of calling "balls" and "strikes" is, that of judging of baulks. The rule—section 7—states that: "The ball must be pitched, not jerked or thrown, to the bat; and whenever the pitcher moves with the apparent purpose or pretension to deliver the ball, he shall so deliver it, and must have neither foot in advance of the front line or off the ground at the time of delivering the qall; and if he fails in either of these particulars then it shall be declared a baulk."

It will be seen by the above rule that there are four

distinct actions of the pitcher, each of which constitutes a "baulk," viz., *jerking* the ball ; *throwing* the
ball ; *making any movement* with the apparent intent
to deliver the ball without delivering it, and having
either foot outside of the lines of his position, or off
the ground, while in the act of delivering the ball.
Now the first thing to be done is to define what a jerk
or a throw is, as the other actions are easily defined.
The following are correct definitions :

WHAT A JERK IS.—A ball is "jerked"—in the meaning of the above rule—when an additional impetus is
given the ball by any portion of the arm touching the
side of the pitcher in the act of delivery. If the arm
does not touch the side of the pitcher the ball is not
jerked. Next as to a thrown ball:

WHAT A THROWN BALL IS.—The ordinary way of
throwing a ball is over the shoulder, but a ball can also
be thrown "underhand," that is, delivering it from the
hand about knee-high or even lower. A ball, however,
cannot be "thrown"—in the meaning of the rule—
either by high or low delivery, unless the elbow is bent
and a whip-like movement be given the arm in the act
of delivery ; consequently, if the arm be kept straight,
and is swung in delivering the ball like the movement
of a pendulum, no throw can be made. We next come
to

THE MOVEMENT IN DELIVERING THE BALL.—Every
pitcher has a peculiar style of delivering the ball. Some
—like Faitoute of the Eureka Club, for instance—have
a series of movements in delivery ; others simply have
but a single swing of the arm in delivery. Now these
movements are those which constitute the action
alluded to in the rule, wherein it reads, "*moves* with
the apparent purpose or pretension to deliver the

ball;" and from the period of the commencement of these preliminary movements, to the time of the delivering of the ball, is to be dated a baulk if the ball is not delivered. For instance, suppose a pitcher takes three movements in delivering a ball—and none take less—viz. first, bending his body, then drawing his arm back, and, lastly, swinging it forward to deliver the ball; if he fail to deliver the ball immediately after making either of these movements, a baulk must be called, unasked. As a consequence, the pitcher making the fewest of these preliminary movements is the one most likely to deceive the player running the bases as to his intention to deliver the ball, without making a baulk. The Umpire should bear in mind that no warning is necessary prior to calling a "baulk." We now come to the last point in judging of baulks, and that is in reference to

HAVING BOTH FEET ON THE GROUND, WHEN ABOUT TO PITCH.—The rule in regard to this reads, "or off the ground at the time of delivering the ball." Now the sentence "time of delivering the ball" has been authoritatively defined by the Committee of Rules of the National Association, to mean, the swing of the arm, from the period of commencing to deliver, to the time the ball actually leaves the hand, and during this time both feet must be on the ground. From the above rules it will be seen that whenever a pitcher jerks a ball, throws it, moves to deliver without delivering, or has either feet off the ground immediately preceding delivery, the Umpire must call a baulk unasked and without warning.

TAKING BASES ON BAULKS.—The striker cannot take a base on a baulk, for the reason that he is not considered "a player running the base," until he has struck a fair ball. Section 19, states that the striker "shall be considered the striker until he has made the first base," but this only bears on the case of a player running home when two hands are out, or in reference to players vacating bases.

On Base Play.

IN JUDGING OF BASE PLAY.—From the position occupied by the Umpire in judging of points of play around the bases, it is next to an impossibility for him to avoid making mistakes at times in his decisions ; more latitude, therefore, should be allowed for errors of this kind than in any other instances occurring in a match. The following rules for judging of base play will be found advantageous in aiding the Umpire in rendering correct decisions.

THE FIRST BASE.—The Umpire must bear in mind that the "striker" running to the first base, is not out unless the ball is held on the base by the baseman *before* the striker touches it. If, at the same time, the striker is not out. It must be palpable that the ball was held on the base before the striker reached it, or he is not out.

THE OTHER BASES.—This rule also applies to the other bases, in those cases wherein players are put out on them in a similar manner to that at first base, as in cases of being obliged to return to bases on fly catches or foul balls.

THE BASE BAG IS THE BASE.—The base bag is considered the base, not the post to which it is, or ought to be, fastened ; therefore if "a player running the bases" touches the base bag with any part of his person, he cannot be put out, though the base bag be out of its place.

TOUCHING PLAYERS.—When "judgment" is called on

touching a player in running the bases, the Umpire should judge of the fact of the player's being touched more by the probability of the occurrence, from the proximity of the players to each other, rather than by the action of the base player in attempting to touch his adversary, as base players frequently are guilty of the trick of feigning to touch their opponents in order to deceive the Umpire, when they are fully aware that he is either not within their reach, or has his foot on the base.

TOUCHING BASES.—If a player running the bases fails to touch any base as he runs round, he must return and touch it, and that, too, in the order of his running. Thus, for instance, if in running from first to home base he fails to touch the second base, he must return by the third base—touching it in returning—and go back to the second and touch it, and he can be put out by being touched by the ball before he reaches the second base in returning. Unless so touched, however, he is not out.

RUNNING BASES ON FOUL BALLS.—When a player is running his bases, and a foul ball is called, he must return to the base he left when the ball was struck,—or the one he left before it was struck, if he is running when it is struck—as the rule prohibits any base being made on a foul ball. In thus returning he should stand on the base until the ball is settled in the hands of the pitcher. Umpires should see that this is done, and should be particular in calling "foul" in a loud voice when a player is running his bases. In returning to a base, on a foul ball, he can be put out as at first base.

RUNNING BASES ON FLY BALLS.—When a fair fly ball has been caught, the player running his bases must return to his base he left when the ball was struck, as in the case of a foul ball. In the case of a foul ball, however, he has to wait on the base until the ball is settled in the hands of the pitcher; whereas in the case of a fair fly catch he can leave his base—after returning to it—the moment the ball is settled in the hands of the fielder catching it.

VACATING BASES.—If a player is on the first base when a *fair* ball is struck, he must immediately *vacate* it and run for his second; and if three players are on the bases when a fair ball is struck, each must promptly vacate the base he occupies and run for the next one—all, in such cases, being *forced* from their bases. Except under the above circumstances, however, they are not obliged to leave their bases. Thus, for instance: if there be no player on the first base, but one on the second or third, or both, and a fair ball be struck, neither of the players on the bases are obliged to leave them; and likewise, if there be a player on the first base and one on the third base when a fair ball is struck, it is only the player on the first base who is obliged to vacate his base. When players are thus obliged to vacate bases, they can be put out on the base they have to run to simply by the ball being held on the base before the player reaches it, there being no necessity to touch the player in order to put him out. In the case of players being on the first and third bases, too, when a fair ball is struck, if the ball be passed to the second base, all that is required is that it be held there before the player reaches it; but if the player on the third base is running home when a fair ball is struck, at the same time that the player on the first runs to the second, or if, having passed the second, he be running to the third, the player running home must be touched by the ball when off his base in order to be put out, and both he and the player running from second to third can return to the bases they last left, and can only be put out, in so returning, by being touched with the ball when off the base; but the player running from the first base, under the above circumstances, cannot return but to the second, as he was forced to leave his first base, but not his second. A very pretty point of play—one made by Goldie, of the Mutual Club—can be made when a player is forced from his first base. Thus, for instance : suppose a player is on the first base when a fair ground-ball is struck to short-field or the pitcher, and the player on the first, seeing that he is sure to be put out if he runs to the second base, decides to remain on the first and let the striker be first put out; if the ball in this instance, be sent to the first baseman, and he holds it on the base before the striker reaches it, the striker only is put out; but if, instead of receiving the ball while standing on the base, he receives it off the base, with no part of his person touching the base, and then, first touching the player standing on the base, puts his foot on the base before the striker reaches it—as Goldie did, in the instance we refer to—both players are out ; inasmuch as, until the striker was put out, the player running the bases was forced to vacate the first base, and could be put out by being touched by the ball, even though he was standing on the base, for the reason that he was not legitimately entitled to stand there ; the moment the striker was put out, however, that moment the player on the first ceased to be obliged to vacate his base, and had he been standing on the first base when the ball was first held on the base, and the baseman had *afterwards* touched him, he would not have been out, because the striker would, in that case, have been first out. The point of the play was in receiving the ball off the base in the first instance, then touching the player, and afterwards holding it on the base. In cases of sharp play like this, it is necessary that the umpire should have his wits about him to decide promptly and correctly.

RETURNING TO BASES.—Players running bases, when

required to return to the base just left—as in the case of
foul or fly balls—must return in the same order they
make them. Thus: suppose a player is on the first base
when a long ball is hit to the right or left field, and the
ball looks as if it would strike fair, but the wind makes
it fall foul, and the player, before "foul" can be called,
has reached his third base, and is on his way home; the
moment "foul" is called under these circumstances, he
must return and *touch* the third and second bases, just
the same as he did in running for the home base.

How Bases Must be Made.—Bases must be made
in the order of striking, and when a fair ball is struck
and it is not caught on the fly, the first base, if occupied
by a player, must be vacated, and likewise the second
and third bases if they are occupied, and players may
be put out under these circumstances in the same manner as the striker can be when running to first base.
Thus, for instance, if there is a player on the first base,
when a ball is struck to the short fielder, all the latter
has to do is to pass it to the second baseman, and if
it be held on the base before the player running from
first to second reaches it, the player in question is out;
and if, after the ball is thus held, it be passed quickly to
first base, and held there before the striker reaches that
base, of course the striker is out also, this passing of
the ball in time thus constituting a "double play."
Should three players be on their base when a fair ball is
struck to the short stop, all the fielders have to do is,
first, to pass the ball to the catcher at home base, he to
the third base man, and the latter to the second base
man, and if the ball be held on the base in each instance
before the player running the bases reaches the base he
is obliged to run for, all three are out. But if there be
a player on the second base and one on the third, and a
fair ball be struck to the short field and not caught on

.the fly, neither of the players are obliged to vacate their bases ; in this case the ball must be passed to first base in order to put the striker out. Under no other circumstances than as above enumerated are players forced to vacate their bases.

OBSTRUCTING PLAYERS AND FIELDERS.—In reference to the rule which declares any player out if he "intentionally" obstructs a fielder in catching or stopping a "all, and which gives a player his base if a fielder or base player "intentionally" prevents him from making it, the Umpire, before he gives his decision, must be *sure*, in the first instance, that the player does not wilfully get in the way of the fielder or base player, and secondly that the latter does not wilfully prevent his adversary from making his base. He should not, of course, hesitate in giving his decision, but when he does give it he should not be in doubt on the subject, but feel satisfied that the obstruction was "intentional." The word "intentional" in the rule, refers to actions *which could have been avoided.* For instance, it is required by the rules that a player running the bases should avoid, if possible, running in the way of a fielder while the latter is trying to catch or stop the ball, and it is also incumbent upon the fielder or base player to allow his adversary free access to the base he is running for. When there is any doubt on the subject, the Umpire should decide in favor of the party obstructed. Thus, if a fielder happens to be standing on the line of a base to catch a falling ball, the player, running the bases, has no right to run up against him because he happens to be between him and the base he is running to, for he could run a few feet to one side without being prevented by the fielder from reaching his base by the latter's effort to catch the ball. But this running out of the line of his base must only be done when it

is not to avoid the ball in the hands of a fielder. In regard also to a base-player taking a ball from a fielder,
the former having no right to stand between the player
and the base he is running to, when the ball could be
equally well taken by standing out of the way of his
adversary.   In such instances as these the obstruction
should be regarded as intentional, in the spirit of the
law, from the fact that it could have been avoided,
though perhaps the obstruction was not actually in-
tended.

RUNNING OUT OF THE LINE OF THE BASES.—The Umpire should bear in mind that unless the player running
the bases runs out of the line of the bases to *avoid* the
ball in the hands of a fielder, he is not to be given out.
When a long hit is made and the striker makes a home
run he invariably runs out of the line of his bases, but
he is not therefore liable to be put out for doing it.   It
is only when he does it to avoid the ball that the penalty is to be inflicted.

ON POINTS OF PLAY NOT SEEN.—The Umpire has
no right to take the testimony of players or spectators,
in regard to any play he has not seen, nor has he a right
to decide on any point of play which he has not himself
witnessed.   He alone is the judge of the play, and if
he has not seen a player touched with the ball or a ball
caught, he has no right to decide the player touched or
caught out.   There are cases when the testimony of
hundreds can be accepted, as in the instance of a foul
ball catch outside the circle of spectators, or a fly catch
taken close to the ground in the outer field near the
circle of spectators, when the testimony of those in the
vicinity of the catch may be fully relied on.   But unless
such overwhelming proof be afforded, the Umpire should
only decide on points of play actually seen by himself.

HOW THE STRIKER CAN BE PUT OUT.—The striker

can be put cut on a foul ball, caught either on the fly or bound, and on a fair ball caught on the fly, and by the ball being held on the first base before he reaches it. He can also be put out by being touched by the ball, after he has struck a fair ball and before he reaches his first base.

WHAT CONSTITUTES A FOUL BALL.—A ball, to be foul, must strike the ground, the person of a player, or any other object *behind* the line of the bases, or it is not a foul ball. If it strikes the *line* of the bases it is a *fair* ball ; it must strike behind the line of the bases to be foul. Suppose, for instance, the ball touches the back part of the home base, it becomes a foul ball from the fact that it thereby strikes behind the "range" of the home base, the " range "—or line of the base—starting from the centre of the base. Again—suppose the ball is struck to left or right fields in such a manner that, if not stopped or caught by a fielder, it would strike the ground foul, but that, by the action of the fielder, who is standing within the foul ball line, it touches his hands and rebounds outside the foul ball line, the Umpire must consider it a *fair* ball. Suppose, also, that a ball similarly hit to the right or left fields, touches the branch of a tree or the roof of a house, which object is within the line of the bases, and the ball glances off and falls to the ground, outside those lines, it is also to be considered a fair ball, these objects being considered just the same as the ground in such cases.

SCORING RUNS.—No run can be legitimately recorded until the player running home *touches the home base,* and not then, if two hands are out when he is running home ; and the *striker* be caught out, either on a fair or foul ball, or be put out at first base, the " striker" being considered the striker—in this instance—until he has reached the first base. Should the striker make his

first base, and be immediately put out in running to
either of the other bases, then the player running home,
when two hands are out, can score his run; but not
then, even, unless he touches the base before the player
running the bases is put out, for the moment the player
is put out the innings terminates, and no run can then
be legitimately scored. The Umpire should watch the
ball and the action of the player touching the home base
as closely as possible under these circumstances.

WHEN THE BALL IS DEAD.

NO PLAYER CAN BE PUT OUT ON A DEAD BALL.—
There are several positions of play in the game when
the ball is what is technically termed "dead," and not
in play, and when this is the case no player can be put
out by being touched or caught. For instance, the ball
is "dead" until it is settled in the hands of the pitcher,
after being stopped in any way by the crowd of spectators, or by any one not engaged in the game. Again,
it is "dead," until settled in the hands of the pitcher,
after it has been struck foul, except as far as a fly or
bound catch is concerned, no player running the bases being liable to be put out until after the ball has been held
by the pitcher. It is also "dead," both in regard to the
striker and player running bases, when a "baulk" or a
'ball" is called, until it is again settled in the hands of
the pitcher. Let us illustrate these cases of dead balls

BALLS STOPPED BY SPECTATORS.—When a fair ball is
hit, or when a ball is thrown from one player to another.
the Umpire should watch the ball and see that it is
neither stopped by the crowd or handled by any one not
engaged in the game, for in either case the ball must first
be settled in the hands of the pitcher before it is again
in play. Suppose, for instance, the striker hits a ball to
the third baseman, and he throws it wildly to the first
base, and it goes by the base player and is stopped by

the crowd, the ball cannot be fielded by the fielder who goes after it, to the baseman, or to any other fielder, to put the player running his bases out, unless it has first been settled in the hands of the pitcher. In case of such a wild throw, the point of play is, for the pitcher to run to the point nearest the player running the bases, and there receive the ball from the fielder who has gone after it ; for, until the pitcher has held it, after being stopped by an outsider, the ball is not in play.

A BAULKED BALL.—Should the pitcher move his foot in delivery—thereby making a "baulk"—and the Umpire call a "baulk," until the ball is returned to the pitcher no player can be put out on it, either on three strikes or by being caught on the fly, or on a foul fly or bound catch, the ball being made "dead" by the baulk. Should the baulk made, too, be one from making a false movement, the ball is not in play until the player running his bases has made the base he has to make, reasonable time being allowed for his making it. Should the striker hit the baulked ball fair, he can take his base on it, just as if he was on a base, as he thereby becomes a player running the bases.

A FOUL BALL.—In the case of a foul ball, struck when a player is running his bases, the player can walk back to his base, even if the baseman has the ball in hand on the base the player has to return to, unless the ball has been in the pitcher's hands first. For instance, suppose a player on the third base, or running home, when a foul ball is struck to left field, and the ball be thrown in by the fielder to the third baseman, and the latter touch the player while he is off the base, instead of first sending the ball to the pitcher, the player, of course, is *not out.* The point of play, in this case, is, for the pitcher to run to the third base and receive the ball from the fielder, and if he holds it before the player can get back to the base the player is out, and that, too, without being touched.

ON THREE STRIKES.—Should a "baulk" be called by the Umpire—say on account of the pitcher moving his foot, for instance—and the striker strikes at the ball for the third time, and misses it, and it be caught on the bound by the catcher, the striker is *not out*, as the ball, the moment the "baulk" was called, was made "dead," and not in play. Again, should the Umpire call a "ball," and the striker strike at it, and hit it fair, and it be caught on the fly, or sent to first base and there held, the striker is *not out*, as the moment the "ball" was called, the ball ceased to be in play. Again, too, in the case of a fly or foul "tip," the same result follows if the Umpire call a "baulk" or a "ball." In fact, no player can be put out, in such case, until after the ball has been returned to and held by the pitcher, after the "baulk" has been made on the "ball" called, the ball, under such circumstances, being considered as "dead," and not in play, just as it is in the case of a foul ball when a player is running his bases, no player running the bases being liable to be put out until the pitcher has first held the ball after "foul" has been called.

PLAYING INTO THE DARK.

PLAYING GAMES INTO THE DARK.—There is no more difficult, and certainly no more unpleasant, duty of an Umpire than that of deciding when a game shall be called, when it has been played until darkness has set in. In the first place there is no rule that could be adopted which would obviate the difficulty except perhaps that of requiring a game to be commenced at noon, and therefore the discretionary power of calling a game is necessarily left in the hands of the Umpire. Secondly, in close contests between rival Clubs, when the issue of the match is important, experience has shown that no Club is free from the tendency to allow their desire to win, to overcome their innate love of fair play under such circumstances ; and hence we find that in just such contests, when the last innings of the game is being played after sun set, the party who lead the score on the last even innings, if in the field, are far too apt to be seized with a fit of short sightedness, and if at the bat either to be over particular in the character of the balls they want pitched to them, or, if two hands are out, and there is no chance of closing the innings before it really becomes too dark to play, they have a great tendency to imagine unfair balls just the thing to suit them ; the result being that they wilfully strike out. Now the Umpire, being expressly declared the sole judge of fair and unfair play in the game, as such a judge possesses an arbitrary power in deciding on disputed points, which nothing but the express wording of any special law can overrule ; and hence, under such circumstances in a match as occur when wilfully unfair play is shown, by either party, either purposely to delay a game, or to hasten its close, as the interests of either of the contesting clubs may require, the Umpire should avail himself of this arbitrary power to nullify the unfair play as much as possible ; and to assist him in his decisions ; in this respect, we give below a few rules which experience has shown to be necessary to be followed in order to put a stop to the unmanly and discreditable style of play known as " playing a game into the dark."

FIRST.—If the party at the bat lead the score on the last even innings played, and are just finishing the first part of the following innings, and it is evident that there is no time to play the inning out ; or if the game is in that position when it is manifestly to their advantage to throw it back to the even innings played, and in order to do so it becomes necessary for their players to get out soon as they can—say, for instance, by striking out—the Umpire, when he sees a batsman strike at a ball either too far off, too high, or too low for him to hit, should refuse to call strikes on him, and this he can legally do, for unless a ball be fairly delivered to the bat, it is not a ball to call strikes on.

SECOND.—If the party in the field are so situated in regard to the issue of the contest as to make it a "point of play" for them to prolong the innings as much as possible, or to have the game "called" on the last even innings played, and the Umpire perceives that they do not field balls which ought to be fielded, or that their pitcher is purposely delivering unfair balls in order to delay the game until it is clearly too dark to play, he may consider every ball within possible reach of the bat as a fair ball, and justly call strikes on the batsman when he strikes at such balls and fails to hit them.

THIRD.—When a game is in the position above described, and the fielders contend that they cannot see the ball, if the Umpire finds that it is light enough for him to distinctly follow the ball with his eye, from the bat to the field, he should allow the game to proceed; but the moment he cannot do so, he should call the game without regard to the position the respective contestants are placed in. He alone must judge of the matter, and he should not take testimony from either side as to its being too dark or otherwise.

NO LAW OF THE GAME CAN BE IGNORED.—If the Umpire perceives, during the progress of a match, that any special rule of the game is being mutually ignored by the contesting clubs, he should at once retire from the field, and proclaim the game as *null* and *void;* for rule 38 states that "Any match game played by any club, in contravention of the rules adopted by this Association, shall be considered null and void, and shall not be counted in the list of match games won or lost." Should rain or any sufficient cause require a postponement of a match, the same can be "put off by mutual consent of the parties about engaging in a game."

OTHER DUTIES.

NO GAME TO BE COMMENCED IN THE RAIN.—Rule 38 expressly prohibits a match game from being commenced in the rain. Should it rain at the time appointed to commence play in a match, the contesting clubs can mutually agree to postpone the game to some other day.

WHEN PLAY CAN BE SUSPENDED.—The power to "call" a game at any time—that is, to suspend play entirely—is left in the hands of the Umpire. If from any just cause a game cannot be concluded, it shall be decided by the last even innings played—provided five innings have been played—and the party having the greatest number of runs shall be declared the winner. It will be seen by section 33 of the rules that it is discretionary with the Umpire when a game shall terminate, of course providing that there is any legitimate cause of interruption : such as a fall of rain, the interference of a crowd of spectators, or the approach of darkness. The law says, "if the game cannot be concluded," this sentence of course limiting the discretionary power of the Umpire to a legitimate point of the game, such for instance as rain or darkness, &c.

REVERSING DECISIONS.—When once a decision has been made it should never be reversed, unless the error is immediately palpable to the Umpire. But if arising from any explanation made by either of the contesting parties, no reversal should follow. Of course in a case where the Umpire makes an illegal decision, and his error in ruling is promptly made apparent, he will be justified in correcting himself in the matter. But, as a general thing, hold to the decision made. No error in ruling on a disputed point should be corrected, or any decision reversed, after the ball has been delivered fairly to the batsman after the occurrence of the point of play in dispute.

DISMISSING TRANSGRESSORS.—The Umpire has the power to order the dismissal of any player from a nine in a match, if he ascertains that any one of the players is either interested in any *bet* made upon the result, or that he is a *member of another club*, or that he has *not* been a member of the club he plays with for the required thirty days prior to the game he plays in, or if he is *paid for his services as a player* in the game he takes part in.

WHO CAN ACT AS UMPIRE.—No one can act as Umpire in a match, played by clubs belonging to the National Association, unless he is a member of a club belonging to and governed by the rules thereof.

NAMING THE WINNING CLUB.—The Umpire, before leaving the ground, must record the name of the winning club in the score books of both the contesting clubs, over his own signature. Until such record is made no club can claim the ball won in a match.

HOW TO SCORE IN BASE BALL.

To score a game of base ball is a simple thing to do, provided the batting only be recorded; but if the particulars of the fielding be required, then more work is necessary. Below will be found the regular system of scoring endorsed by the National Association, and practised by all the best scorers in the country.

TO SCORE THE BATTING.

When the players take their positions in the field, and the game commences, all the scorer has to do to record the particulars of the batting, is, the moment a run is secured, to put down a dot (.) in the corner of the square opposite the name of the batsman making the run; and when an out is made all he has to do is to mark down the figure 1, for the put out, 2 for the second out, and 3 for the third. By way of checking the score, he can also record each run at the end of the score of each batsman, so that the batsman's total score at the end of each innings can be seen at a glance.

When the innings terminates, add up the total dots or runs recorded, and mark the figure underneath the column of the inning, and underneath this figure, record the grand total at the close of each innings. Thus, suppose 3 runs are scored in the 1st inning, and 2 in the 2d and 3 in the 3d, under the total figure of the 2d innings you mark down 5, and under the total figure of the 3d innings you mark down the figure 8; by this means you can tell at a glance what the total score of a player or of an innings is at any time during the game. The above is simply the method of scoring the runs and outs made, without the particulars of the fielding.

TO SCORE THE FIELDING.

To record the manner in which each player is out requires a system of abbreviations, and the following is the one now in general use, and endorsed by the National Association. The abbreviations used are very simple, and are easily remembered. For instance A,

B and C stand for the 1st, 2d and 3d bases, and for recording everything else, the first or last letter of the word to be abbreviated, is used. Thus for the word "fly," the letter F is used ; for the word "bound," the letter D is used, because B, the first letter of the word, is used to designate the 2d base. For the word "foul," L is used because F represents "fly." Now these are the fundamental abbreviations used to record the majority of outs in a match, and by way of illustration we will proceed to score a game, using simply the above abbreviations.

A GAME SCORED.

In recording the fielding score of a game, it is first necessary that each batsman and fielder's name be designated by a figure, and they are numbered from one to nine, in the order in which they strike. The accompanying diagram will illustrate this order, and an explanation of the abbreviations used in it will be found in the account of the game which follows. The score record is that of the Union Club in their match with the Eckford's, June 6th, 1866 :

(SEE TABLE ON NEXT PAGE.)

Now, the above is a complete record of the batting of the Unions and the fielding of the Eckford's in the above match, and the explanation of the abbreviations used are as follows :

Smith was the first striker, and went out on three strikes, which is recorded by the figure "1" for the first out, and the letter K to indicate how put out, K being the last letter of the word "struck." The letter K is used in this instance as being easier to remember in connection with the word struck than S, the first letter, would be.

BATSMEN.	1	2	3	4	5	6	7	8	9	FIELDERS.
1 Smith, 1st B.	k5 LF 3									1 Grum, C. F.
2 Abrams, 3d B.	4 A 2		3d		1 F 1					2 Brown, 2d B.
3 Birdsall, C.			2-4 A 1		8-2 B 2			4 A 2		3 Zettlein, P.
4 Martin, 2d B.	3d		8-2 B 3		2-4 A 3		3d			4 Klein, 1st B.
5 Pabor, P.	5 T D 3	5 LF 2	5 LF 5 L D 1				2-4 A 1	4 F 3 LF 2 3		5 Beach, C.
6 Ketchum, C. F.		1 F 1		8-4 A 2		2 P 7-5 H 2 3			6-4 A 1	6 Mills, 3d B.
7 Akin, L. F.			5 LF 3	5 LF 3		5 LF 3		5 LF 8 F 1 2		7 Swandell, R. F.
8 Bassford, R. F.		5-6 C 2					2-4 A 1		7 F 3	8 McDonald, S. S.
9 Hannegan, S. S.										9 Ryan, L. F.
Total,	1	2	0	0	3	0	5	4	0	
Grand total,	3	3	3	3	6	6	11	15	15	

Abrams was second striker and second out, and was put out at first base by Klein, and this is recorded by the figure " 2 " for second out, and the figure " 4 " for Klein—he being 4th on the list of the Eckford nine—with the letter A for 1st base. Birdsall then scored a run, and this is recorded by a dot in the corner of the square. Martin was on his 3d base, when Pabor went out on a tip-bound, and this is recorded first by placing the small figure and letter " 3d " in the corner of Martin's square, and then in Pabor's the figure " 3 " for 3d out, and the small figure " 5 " for Beach's name, and the letters T (for tip), D for tip bound. The total score of the innings being one run, which is recorded at the bottom of the column of the first innings.

Ketchum was the first striker in the 2d innings, and he was caught on the fly by Grum, recorded thus, " 1 F." Akin then made a run—recorded with a dot ; Bassford was put out at 3d base by Beach and Mills, recorded by the figures 5 (for Beach, who threw the ball,) and 6 (for Mills, who touched the player). Hannegan then made a run—another dot—and Smith was caught out on a foul fly by Beach, recorded by the figure 5 (for Beach) and letters L F for foul fly. Two runs were scored in this innings, and 2 is the figure recorded at the foot of the column, the figure 3 being placed underneath to indicate the grand total at the close of the 2d innings.

It is scarcely necessary to further describe the score, as by this time the reader will have learnt how to follow it out himself. This score includes nearly all the abbreviations used in a game ; but sometimes more are used, and the following list, with their definitions, will be found complete for recording every particular of the game :

A for first base.

B for second base.

C for third base.

H for home base.

F for catch on the fly.

D for catch on the bound.

L for foul balls.

T for tips.

K for struck out.

R for run out between bases.

Double letters—H R, or h r, for home runs.

L F for foul ball on the fly.

L D for foul ball on the bound.

T F for tip on the fly.

T D for tip on the bound.

. for a run ; 1st, 2d or 3d for left on bases according to the base.

" Foul fly " or " foul bound " catches are those made from high balls in the air. " Tip fly " or " tip bound " catches are those made from foul balls sharp from the bat to the catcher.

SCORING.

Hints to Scorers

PASSED BALLS are those that are missed by the catcher, thereby admitting of the player running a base ; none but those on which bases are run are counted as passed balls.

HOME RUNS are made when the batsman goes the round of the bases and reaches home before being touched with the ball. In the first place, however, no home run can be fairly scored if the player running home is obliged to stop on any of the three bases to avoid being put out. Of course it does not follow in all cases that, because he does not stop on the bases in running round, that he thereby makes a home run. In recording home runs, only score runs as home runs which are made from hits to the outer field, out of the reach of the fielders, on which the home base is made by the striker before the ball is returned to the catcher, or passes the home base. These are what is called clean home runs, and are the only runs of the kind meriting a special record. Home runs made from errors in the field, in the way of gross failures to stop a ball or from wild throws, should not be counted.

STRIKING OUT, is when a batsman strikes three times at a ball, and failing to hit it is either caught out by the catcher, or put out at the first base. In both cases it is recorded as "struck out," and not as being out from the catch or at the base.

FLY CATCHES.—Under this head every fly catch is recorded, whether foul or fair.

FOUL BALLS.—Fly or bound catches, either from foul balls or "tips," are all included under the head of "foul balls."

MISSED CATCHES.—Charge a catch as missed, if the ball touches the fielder's hands and he fails to hold it.

LEFT ON BASES.—The number of times a player is left on bases, should be recorded, as it frequently happens that a good hit fails to be rewarded with a run, from the fault of the striker following the one making the hit.

RUN OUT.—When a player is put out between the bases, from being touched, he is charged with being "run out," and the credit of the fielding goes to the player touching him.

RUNS NOT TO BE SCORED.—No player running home at the time the ball is struck, when two hands are out, can score his run if the striker be put out either on the fly or at first base. Neither is a player running home, when two hands are out, entitled to score his run unless he touches the base before the third hand is out.

THE MODEL BASE BALL PLAYER.

This is an individual not often seen on a ball ground, but he nevertheless exists; and as a description of his characteristics will prove advantageous, we give a pen photograph of him in the hope that his example will be followed on all occasions, for if it were, an end would at once be put to many actions which now give rise to unpleasantness on our ball grounds.

HIS MORAL ATTRIBUTES.

The principal rule of action of our model base ball player is, to comport himself like a gentleman on all occasions, but especially on match days, and in so doing he abstains from *profanity* and its twin and vile brother obscenity, leaving these vices to be alone cultivated by graduates of our penitentiaries.

He always has his temper under control, and takes everything good humoredly, or, if angered at all, makes an effort and keeps silent.

He never censures errors of play made by a brother member or an opponent, as he is well aware that fault-finding not only leads to no improvement in the play of the one who blunders, but on the contrary is calculated to have the very reverse effect.

He was never known to dispute the decision of an Umpire, for knowing the peculiar position an Umpire is placed in, he is careful never to wound his feelings by implying that his judgment is weak, his partiality apparent, or his integrity of character doubtful, one or other of these imputations being made whenever that official's decision is disputed by a player. Moreover, he is never guilty of questioning the decision of the Umpire by his *actions*, which, in many instances, are as expressive in this respect as words ; but, when judgment has been rendered, he silently acquiesces in the decision, whatever it may be.

He never takes an ungenerous advantage of his opponents, but acts towards them as he would wish them to act towards himself. Regarding the game as a healthful exercise, and a manly and exciting recreation, he plays it solely for the pleasure it affords him, and if victory crowns his efforts in a contest, well and good ; but should defeat ensue he is equally ready to applaud the success obtained by his opponents ; and by such action he robs defeat of half its sting, and greatly adds to the pleasure the game has afforded both himself and his adversaries.

He never permits himself to be pecuniarily interested in a match, for knowing the injurious tendency of such a course of action to the best interests of the game, he values its welfare too much to make money an object in view in playing ball.

He is ever prompt in his engagements, is punctually in attendance on the field on match days ; readily obeys the commands of the presiding officer of the day ; plays the game throughout, whether winning or losing, to the best of his ability, and retires from the field apparently content with the result whatever it may be.

He abides by every rule of the game, as long as it is legally in force; if it should not meet with his approval he awaits the proper time to have it erased from the statute books ; but he never ignores its existence as long as it is legally a rule of the game.

HIS PHYSICAL QUALIFICATIONS.

The physical qualifications of our model player are as follows. To be able to throw a ball with accuracy of aim a dozen or a hundred yards.

To be fearless in facing and stopping a strongly batted or thrown ball.

To be able to catch a ball either on the "fly" or bound, either within an inch or two of the ground, or eight or ten feet from it, with either the right or left hand or both.

To be able to run swiftly, and to check himself suddenly, and to pick up a ball while running.

To be able to hit a swiftly pitched ball or a "slow twister" with equal skill, and also to command his bat so as to hit the ball either within six inches of the ground or as high as his shoulder, and either towards the right, centre or left fields, as occasion may require.

To be able to occupy any position on the field creditably, but to excel in one position only.

To be familiar, practically and theoretically, with every rule of the game and "point" of play.

To conclude our description of a model base ball player, we have to say, that his conduct is as much marked by courtesy of demeanor and liberality of action as it is by excellence in a practical exemplification of the beauties of the game ; and his highest aim is to characterize every contest in which he may be engaged, with conduct that will mark it as a trial as to which party excels in the moral attributes of the game, as it is one that decides any question of physical superiority.

HOW TO ORGANIZE A CLUB.

In organizing a club, it should be remembered that the Constitution of the National Association requires each Club entering the Association to be composed of not less than eighteen active members, that is, men who actively engage in play on practice days, and who take part in match games.

The corps of officers requisite consists of a President, Secretary, and Treasurer. A Club can, of course, add a Vice-President and Corresponding Secretary.

Honorary members of Clubs can also act as active members, in being appointed delegates and representatives; the privilege of voting at meetings, however, is denied them.

It is desirable to secure the services of one or two men in a Club who will take as much interest in its welfare as if it was a pet stock company, yielding them large pecuniary returns. Without such supporters, no club will flourish long as a general thing.

Don't elect bad tempered men in your club, no matter how noted as players they may be. Leave them out, for they will eventually do more injury to a club than benefit.

We append the Constitution and By-Laws of the National Club, of Washington, as a good model to copy from in organizing a new Club. They are as follows :

CONSTITUTION.

ARTICLE I.

Sec. 1. This Club shall be known as the " National Base Ball Club of Washington ;" and the objects of the Club shall be to " improve, prosper, and perpetuate the American game of Base-Ball," and advance morally, socially, and physically, the interests of its members.

ARTICLE II.

Sec. 1. Candidates for membership must be proposed in writing, to the Board of Directors, by a member of the Club, setting forth the name and address of the candidate, and be signed by the member offering the same.

Sec. 2. Such proposition must be accompanied with the initiation fee and annual dues, and be before the Board at least one week for consideration. The Directors shall report the same at the next meeting of the Club thereafter, with their opinions thereon, and the candidate must be balloted for; and if no more than one-third of the members dissent, he shall be declared elected.

Sec. 3. Honorary members may be elected by a unanimous vote at any regular meeting of the Club.

Sec. 4. Any member desiring to withdraw from the Club shall offer his resignation in writing, at a regular meeting, and such resignation may be accepted if the member be not in arrears.

Sec. 5. Any member who shall make himself obnoxious, or be guilty of disreputable conduct, or violate any of the rules and regulations of the Club, may by a two-third vote at any regular meeting be expelled, suspended, reprimanded, or fined.

ARTICLE III.

OFFICERS.

Sec. 1. The officers of this Club shall consist of a President, Vice-President, Secretary, Treasurer, and a Board of five Directors, "one of whom shall be the President," who shall be elected on the first Monday of March in each year, and shall hold their offices for one year, or until their successors are respectively elected.

Sec. 2. Each "officer" shall be elected by ballot separately, and must receive a majority of all the votes cast.

Sec. 3. The Board of Directors may be balloted for

conjointly, and the four candidates receiving the greatest number of votes cast shall be declared elected.

SEC. 4. In case of vacancy in any office by reason of resignation of any officer, or for any other cause, the same shall be filled at a regular meeting.

ARTICLE IV.

DUTIES OF OFFICERS.

SEC. 1. It shall be the duty of the President to preside at all meetings of the Club, preserve order, and appoint all committees not otherwise provided for.

SEC. 2. The Vice-President shall perform all the duties of the President in his absence.

SEC. 3. The Secretary shall keep a correct record of the proceedings of the Club, notify members of all special meetings, and keep a correct register of the members, with their places of business or residence. He shall keep a debit and credit account with each member, shall receive all moneys paid to the Club, and report the amount of the same at any regular meeting, and hand the same to the Treasurer, taking his receipt therefor. He shall also prepare, and cause to be published, notices of meetings, match games, and such other matter as may be ordered by the Directors.

SEC. 4. The Treasurer shall keep in a suitable book an account of all moneys received and paid : shall pay all bills against the Club, when instructed so to do by the Board of Directors, or by a vote of the Club, and when called upon shall state the amount of funds on hand " at any regular meeting."

SEC. 5. The Directors shall provide all implements required by the Club, and suitable grounds for exercise ; they shall audit all bills against the Club, and when correct direct the payment of the same by written order on the Treasurer. When any match shall have been agreed on by the Club, they shall select the nines, appoint captains, and have entire control of the same, and make all necessary arrangements therefor; they shall place no player on the first nine who refuses to play on any inferior nine.

ARTICLE V.

INITIATION FEE, DUES, ETC.

SEC. 1. Each member shall pay "on joining," as an initiation fee, the sum of *five dollars.*

SEC. 2. The annual dues shall be five dollars, payable in advance, on or before the first regular meeting in May. Members joining after the month of June will pay *pro rata* of the above dues.

SEC. 3. No member in arrears, or who has continued in arrears for the period of thirty days, (after 1st May,) shall be allowed to participate in any game or meeting of the Club, and if not then settled, his name shall be erased from the Club Books.

SEC. 4. Should the funds of this Club at any time become exhausted, there shall be an equal assessment on each member to obtain such sum as may be required; such assessment to be made by a majority of the members present at a regular meeting.

ARTICLE VI.

MEETINGS.

SEC. 1. There shall be an annual meeting of the Club on the first Monday of March in each year, and a regular meeting on the first Mo day of each month, at such place as the President shall designate; and all meetings shall commence at 7½ o'clock P. M.

SEC. 2. The President may call special meetings for business when he shall deem it necessary, and also at the written request of any five members.

SEC. 3. Seven members shall constitute a quorum for the transaction of business at any meeting.

SEC. 4. The regular meetings for field exercise shall be on Monday, Wednesday, and Friday, of each week during the season, at such hour as the Directors may designate.

SEC. 5. There shall be a practice game between the first and second nines one day of each week, at such time as the Directors may designate.

ARTICLE VII.

AMENDMENTS.

SEC. 1. No alteration or amendment of this Constitution, or the by-laws herewith of this Club, shall be made except by a two-third vote of all the members present at a regular meeting; nor then, unless such alteration or amendment shall have been submitted in writing at a regular meeting at least one month previous to its adoption.

BY-LAWS.

ARTICLE I.

RULES AND REGULATIONS FOR FIELD EXERCISE.

SEC. 1. This Club shall be governed by the following rules and regulations in all exercise games :

Rule 1. When assembled for field exercise the presiding officer shall appoint a scorer, and designate two members as captains, who shall retire and make up the game to be played, and shall observe at the same time that the players put opposite to each other should be as nearly equal as possible. The choice of sides shall then be tossed for; and the first " at bat" shall be decided in like manner.

Rule 2. In making up a game for exercise, if there are fourteen or more players of this Club present on the field, no other persons, not members of this Club, shall be chosen in ; but if there are not fourteen members present, the members of other Clubs may be chosen in to make up eighteen players in all.

Rule 3. Members appearing after the game has commenced, shall not be chosen in if there is no vacancy, or the sides full.

Rule 4. The scorer shall keep the game in a book provided for that purpose; and shall note all violations of the by-laws, rules and regulations, during exercise. He shall decide all disputes and differences relative to the game in the absence of the Umpire, from which decision there shall be no appeal.

Rule 5. The captains shall have absolute direction of their sides, and shall designate the position each player shall occupy in the field, which cannot be changed without their consent.

SEC. 2. All exercise and match games shall be governed by the rules and regulations adopted by the National Convention of Base Ball Clubs held in the City of New York.

ARTICLE II.

RESTRICTIONS.

SEC. 1. It shall not be " lawful," and shall be deemed to be a violation of these By-laws—

For any member to use improper or profane language at *any* meeting of the Club, or during the progress of any game;

For wearing or using the apparel of a fellow member without his permission;

For disputing the decision of an Umpire during field exercise;

For audibly expressing his opinion on a doubtful play before the decision of an Umpire is given;

For refusing to obey his captain in the exercise of his lawful authority;

For leaving a meeting, when assembled for business or exercise, without the permission of the presiding officer.

ARTICLE III.

ORDER OF BUSINESS.

1. Reading of minutes.
2. Reports of officers.
3. Reports of committees.
4. Election of officers.
5. Election of members.
6. Dues and finances.
7. Unfinished business.
8. Miscellaneous business.
9. Adjournment.

The order of business as above arranged may at any time, for an occasion, be changed or dispensed with by a two-third vote of the members present at a meeting.

Parliamentary rules shall be observed at all meetings of the Club.

Best Averages of Each Club for 1865.

ACTIVE.

PLAYERS.	MATCHES.	OUTS.	AVE-RAGE.	RUNS.	AVE-RAGE.	CLEAR SCORES.	BLANK SCORES.
Page,	15	36	2— 6	58	3—13	0	0
Rooney,	16	41	2— 9	46	2—14	0	2
Kelley,	16	42	1—10	44	2—12	1	1

ATHLETIC.

McBride,	15	31	2— 1	60	4— 0	1	2
Berkenstock,	15	38	2— 8	59	3—14	0	1
Reach,	15	44	2—14	57	3—12	0	1

ATLANTIC.

Start,	18	39	2—3	82	4—10	0	0
C. Smith,	15	38	2—8	65	4— 5	0	0
Crane,	18	42	2—6	71	3—17	1	0

EAGLE.

Collins,	8	16	2—0	19	2—8	1	2
Slote,	8	18	2—2	19	2—3	0	1
Doremus,	6	16	2—4	14	2—2	0	0

ECKFORD.

Farrall,	7	16	2—2	24	3—3	1	1
A. Mills,	11	23	2—1	35	3—2	0	0
Grum,	9	24	2—6	28	3—1	0	0

ECLECTIC.

Dr. Bell,	5	8	1—3	25	5—0	1	0
Clarke,	5	9	1—4	25	5—0	0	0
M. Humphrey,	5	13	2—3	17	3—2	0	0

EMPIRE.

PLAYERS.	MATCHES.	OUTS.	AVE-RAGE.	RUNS.	AVE-RAGE.	CLEAR SCORES.	BLANK SCORES.
Waterman,	13	26	2—0	43	3—4	1	0
Russell,	5	13	2—3	18	3—3	0	0
Kelley,	14	35	2—7	45	3—3	0	1

ENTERPRISE.

E. Smith,	11	23	2—1	45	4—1	2	0
Jewell,	8	20	2—4	31	2—7	1	0
R. Cornwell,	7	21	3—0	25	3—4	0	0

EUREKA.

Fryatt,	5	15	3—0	21	4— 6	0	1
Callaway,	14	42	3—0	52	3—10	0	2
Brientnall,	13	35	2—9	43	3— 4	0	2

EXCELSIOR.

Flanly,	6	14	2—2	25	4—1	0	0
Clyne,	7	22	3—1	26	3—5	0	0
Brainard,	7	20	2—6	30	3—4	1	0

GOTHAM.

H. Wright,	7	16	2—2	22	3—1	0	0
Dockney,	9	25	2—7	26	2—8	1	2
Hatfield,	7	20	2—6	16	2—2	0	1

HUDSON RIVER.

Adams,	11	25	2—3	45	4—1	0	1
Mapes,	12	32	2—8	43	3—7	0	2
Milspaugh,	8	22	2—6	30	3—6	0	0

KNICKERBOCKER, OF NEW YORK.

Hinsdale,	5	8	1—3	19	3—4	1	0
Kissam,	5	9	1—4	16	3—1	0	0
Taylor,	5	15	3—0	16	3—1	0	0

KNICKEROCKER, OF ALBANY.

Lamoure,	5	12	2—2	16	3—1	0	0
Bliss,	6	18	3—3	19	2—2	0	0
Carey,	6	17	2—5	17	2—5	0	0

KEYSTONE.

Cope,	11	23	2— 1	34	3—1	1	1
Frazier,	7	17	2— 3	22	3—1	0	0
Cuthbert,	12	23	1—11	33	2—9	1	1

MUTUAL.

PLAYERS.	MATCHES.	OUTS.	AVE-RAGE.	RUNS.	AVE-RAGE.	CLEAR SCORES.	BLANK SCORES.
Brown,	11	29	2—7	34	3—1	1	0
McMahon,	15	36	2—6	43	2—13	0	0
Goldie,	13	34	2—8	38	2—12	0	1

MYSTIC.

Reynolds	8	18	2—2	23	2—7	0	1
C. Glover,	8	22	2—6	20	2—4	0	1
Manson,	8	26	3—2	17	2—1	0	1

NATIONAL.

Prouty,	5	12	2—2	18	3—3	1	0
Parker,	5	13	2—3	16	3—1	0	0
Berthrong,	5	12	2—2	13	2—3	0	0

NEWARK.

Terrell,	5	11	2—1	12	2—2	0	1
Thorne,	5	16	3—1	12	2—2	0	1
Bailey,	5	16	3—1	8	1—3	0	0

PIONEER.

Dunlap,	5	13	2—3	16	3—1	1	1
Walters,	6	17	2—5	18	3—0	0	0
Hoagland,	5	14	2—4	13	2—3	0	2

RESOLUTE.

M. Rogers,	5	13	2—3	18	3—3	0	0
Lockwood,	7	19	2—5	16	2—2	0	0
J. Wilson,	5	16	3—1	12	2—3	0	0

STAR.

Mitchell,	5	8	1—3	26	5—1	2	0
McDiarmed,	5	12	2—2	21	4—1	0	0
Thomson,	6	15	2—3	23	3—5	0	0

UNION.

Hudson,	19	46	2—8	63	3—6	1	2
Smith,	21	53	2—11	65	3—2	2	3
Hannegan,	21	55	2—13	64	3—1	3	2

SECRETARIES AND THEIR ADDRESSES.

Active of New York.............W. J. Rooney, 19 Mulberry
       street, New York.
Alert of Philadelphia, Pa...... J. R. Peterson, care of *City
       Item*, Phila.
Americus of Newark, N. J.......John Cotter, Newark P. O.
Athletic of Philadelphia, Pa....P. S. Bell, 609 Walnut St.,
       Philadelphia.
Atlantic of Brooklyn, L. I ......S. Smith, Box 214 P. O.,
       Brooklyn.
Contest of Brooklyn, N. Y......Care of Brooklyn Union.
Clinton of Brooklyn, N. Y.......   "   "   "
Camden of Philadelphia, Pa....J. Evans, care of *City Item*,
       Philadelphia.
Charter Oak of Hartford, Conn.F. M. Blair, P. O., Hartford.
Constellation of Brooklyn.......Union Ball Grounds, Brook-
       lyn, E. D.
Eagle of New York.............M. A. Kelly, County Clerk's
       Office.
Eclectic of New York...........M. Engles, Box 5622 P. O.,
       New York.
Empire of New York............T. Kelley, County Clerk's
       Office.
Eckford of Brooklyn, N. Y......G. F. Gosman, 44 Wall St.,
       N. Y.
Enterprise of Brooklyn, N. Y....E. M. Jewell, 4 Fulton St.,
       Brooklyn.
Equity of Philadelphia, Pa......C. G. Hancock, care of
       City Item, Phila.
Eon of Portland, Me........ ....Frank W. Smith, Box 1764,
       Portland, Me.
Eureka of Newark, N. J.........C. C. Momas, P.O., Newark.
Excelsior of Brooklyn, N. Y.....C. J. Holt, 50 Exchange
       Place, N. Y.
Fulton Market of New York.....J. Murphy, 310 Pearl St.,
       N. Y.

Gotham of New York..........C. E. Beadle, P. O., Hoboken.

Hudson River of Newburgh, N.Y.L. B. Halsey, P. O., Newburgh.

Harvard of Cambridge, Mass...Harvard College.

Independent of Brooklyn, N.Y..C. H. Edwards, care of J. M. Hartshorne & Bro., 55 Exchange Place, N. Y.

Irvington of Irvington, N. J....J. M. C. Eaton, P. O., Irvington, Essex Co., N. J.

Jefferson of New York....... .T. Callan, Perry's Hotel, Hoboken.

Jefferson of Washington........P. O., Washington

Keystone of Philadelphia, Pa....F. A. Frazier, Box 1068 P. O., Phila.

Knickerbocker of New York....C. A. Righim, 38 Murray.

Knickerbocker of Albany, N. Y..W. R. Dorlon, Box 49 P.O., Albany, N. Y.

Lowell of Boston, Mass.........J. A. Sawell, Washington street, Boston.

Liberty of New Brunswick, N. J.J. Leupp, P.O., New Brunswick.

Mountain of Altoona, Pa.... ...Penn. Railroad Co.'s Office, Altoona, Pa.

Mutual of New York...... ....W. H. Dongan, 32 Chambers street, N. Y.

Minerva of Philadelphia, Pa....George G. Esler, care of *City Item*, Phila.

M. M. VanDyke of New York. ..Union Ball Grounds, Brooklyn, E. D.

Mohawk of Brooklyn, N. Y......Geo. P. Molleson, 177 Deane street, Brooklyn.

National of Washington, D. C...M. A. Tappen, Third Auditor's Office, Treasury, Washington, D. C.

National of Albany, N. Y........B. W. Johnson, National Commercial Bank, Albany, N. Y.

National of Jersey City, N. J....J. W. Edwards, 147 York street, Jersey City.

Olympic of Philadelphia, Pa... R. Dusenbery, care of *City Item*, Phila.

Olympic of Paterson, N. J......P. O., Patterson, N. J.

Oriental of Brooklyn, New York.Care of Brooklyn Union.

Pioneer of Newark, N. J........R. B. Butler, P.O., Newark.
Potomac of Washington, D. C...P. O., Washington.
Philadelphia of Philadelphia....J. J. Keyes, care of *City Item*, Phila.
Powhattan of Brooklyn, N. Y...Brooklyn *Union* office.
Peconic of Brooklyn, N. Y.........   "   "   "
Resolute of Brooklyn, N. Y......A. H. Raffen, Brooklyn *Union* office.
Star of Brooklyn, N. Y.........W. R. McDiarmed, 50 Wall street, N. Y.
Social of New York............T. Dewitt, Perry's Hotel, Hoboken.
Surprise of West Farms, N. Y...James W. Graff, Box 3 P.O., West Farms, Westchester Co., N. Y.
Swiftfoot of Philadelphia, Pa...J. C. Addis, care of *City Item*, Phila.
Union of Morrisania, N. Y.......Chas. N. Swift, P. O., Morrisania, N. Y.
Una of Mount Vernon.........P. O., Mount Vernon, Westchester Co., N. Y.
Union of Washington, D. C.....P. O., Washington, D. C.
Unionville of Long Island......Jas. Morris, Unionville, L. I.
Utica of Utica, N. Y............J. M. Thompson, P. O., Utica, N. Y.

www.ingramcontent.com/pod-product-compliance
Lightning Source LLC
Chambersburg PA
CBHW031455270326
41930CB00007B/1008